HOAXED!

FAKES & Mistakes in the World of SCIENCE

By the Editors of *YES Mag*
Illustrated by Howie Woo

Kids Can Press

For my brother Michael, who let me wake him up whenever things went bump in the middle of the night — J.I.

Acknowledgments

Special thanks to: Dr. Jess Brewer, Department of Physics, University of British Columbia; Dr. Jan H. Brunvand, folklorist, professor emeritus, University of Utah; Dr. Yves Candela, Assistant Curator of Invertebrate Palaeontology and Palaeobotany, National Museums Scotland; C.T. Keally, archaeologist specializing in Japanese palaeolithic and Jomon cultures; Dr Alan Knox, Historic Collections, University of Aberdeen, King's College, Scotland; Greg Long, author, *The Making of Bigfoot*; artist John Lundberg, Circlemakers.org; Pat Morris; Dr. Richard A. Muller, Department of Physics, University of California Berkeley; John Nance; Dr. Brian Naranjo, Department of Physics, UCLA; Dr. Jeremy Northcote, School of Marketing, Tourism and Leisure, Faculty of Business and Law, Edith Cowan University, Australia; author and scientist Matt Ridley; Dr. Pamela Rasmussen, Assistant Curator of Mammalogy and Ornithology, Michigan State University Museum; Dr. Miles Russell FSA, Senior Lecturer in Prehistoric and Roman Archaeology, School of Conservation Sciences, Bournemouth University, UK; Dave Thomas, New Mexicans for Science and Reason; Prof. Gretel van Rooyen, Department of Botany, University of Pretoria.

The *YES Mag* team member who worked on this book is Jude Isabella.

Text © 2009 Peter Piper Publishing Inc.
Illustrations © 2009 Kids Can Press

Kids Can Press acknowledges the financial support of the Government of Ontario, through the Ontario Media Development Corporation's Ontario Book Initiative; the Ontario Arts Council; the Canada Council for the Arts; and the Government of Canada, through the BPIDP, for our publishing activity.

Published in Canada by	Published in the U.S. by
Kids Can Press Ltd.	Kids Can Press Ltd.
25 Dockside Drive	2250 Military Road
Toronto, ON M5A 0B5	Tonawanda, NY 14150

www.kidscanpress.com

Edited by Valerie Wyatt and Stacey Roderick
Designed by Julia Naimska
Illustrations by Howie Woo

The hardcover edition of this book is smyth sewn casebound.
The paperback edition of this book is limp sewn with a drawn-on cover.
Manufactured in Singapore, in 2/2011 by Tien Wah Press (Pte) Ltd.

CM 09   0 9 8 7 6 5 4 3 2
CM PA 09   0 9 8 7 6 5 4 3 2

Photo credits appear on page 48.

Library and Archives Canada Cataloguing in Publication

Hoaxed! : fakes and mistakes in the world of science / written by editors of YES mag.

ISBN 978-1-55453-206-3 (bound)
ISBN 978-1-55453-207-0 (pbk.)

1. Fraud in science—Juvenile literature.

Q175.37.H62 2009	j500	C2008-903302-7

Kids Can Press is a *corus*™ Entertainment company

Contents

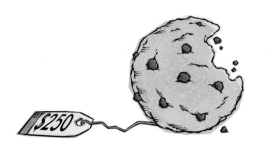

Hoaxes Exposed

Have you ever been hoaxed? Hoaxes are deliberate deceptions that fool people. You could call them lies, on a big scale.

The first known hoaxes happened way back in medieval times. For example, a traveler to some faraway place might come home and swear he had seen a Cyclops or a unicorn or a fire-breathing dragon. Really! And there have been hoaxes ever since. Open a newspaper today, and you can read about someone somewhere trying to pull the wool over other people's eyes.

Hoaxes happen in science, too. But scientists are trained to be skeptical — they simply don't believe everything they see or hear. If someone makes an amazing claim (We can turn lead into gold!), they say, "Prove it!"

To prove something, scientists first come up with an experiment to test their idea, or hypothesis. They do the experiment many

HOAXSPOTTING

Here are some common elements of a hoax. See if you can spot them in the hoaxes you read in this book.

- Dates of "discoveries" are vague.
- There's only one eyewitness.
- A well-known, respected scientist or some kind of "expert" is involved, despite a claim that might otherwise be dismissed.
- Cultural, professional or personal pride is a factor.
- The report of the discovery appears in the media (radio, TV, newspapers, the Internet) before being published in a scientific journal.
- Someone has something to gain — often cash.

times. They know they're on to something if the results of the experiment support their hypothesis. To make sure, they share the information with other scientists, usually by publishing a report in a scientific journal. Other scientists read the report and perform the same experiment. If the experiment works again and again and again, it provides stronger evidence for the hypothesis. One experiment, or one paper, means very little.

That's how it's supposed to work. But scientists are people, too, and sometimes, hoaxes, fakes and mistakes rock their world.

Piltdown Plot Revealed!

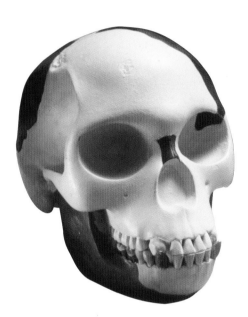

The skull you see here belongs to Piltdown Man, so named because it was dug out of a gravel pit in Piltdown, England, in the early 1900s. Back then, Piltdown Man caused a major sensation. He was called the missing link between apes and humans, something scientists who studied human evolution had been searching for. But not everyone was convinced the skull was the real thing.

Man or Ape?

The skull was found by an amateur scientist named Charles Dawson. In the late 1800s, he had been strolling along the road near the village of Piltdown when he came across a couple of laborers digging gravel out of a pit. Dawson, who knew something about geology, spied some flint. Flint is a kind of rock ancient humans often used for making tools. If you find flint, you may get lucky and also find human remains.

Dawson quizzed the diggers: Did they find any bones? Tools? Nothing. Dawson sifted through the pit himself and asked the men to keep an eye out for anything unusual.

In 1908, Dawson visited the pit again, and a worker handed him a piece of bone. It was a piece of human skull bone. Dawson checked the pit, looking for more remains or tools but found nothing. Almost a year later, he was digging again and found another piece of the skull and a hippopotamus tooth. Later on, more skull fragments were dug up.

In 1912, Dawson sent a letter to Sir Arthur Smith Woodward, a geologist with the Natural History Museum in London. He told Woodward what he had found in Piltdown. Would Sir Woodward join him for a dig? Yes, he certainly would.

Anthropology (the study of people) was a young science at the time. Not long before, Charles Darwin (not to be confused with Charles Dawson) had come up with his revolutionary theory of evolution. It said that all life on Earth, including humans, had descended from a common ancestor. Remains of ancient humans had been found in Germany. In France, evidence of early humans was painted all over the walls of newly found caves. Now Piltdown Man could put England on the anthropological map.

Charles Dawson (left) at the Piltdown site, where he found unusual bone fragments — including a tooth (inset). At the time, scientists thought the remains were 500 000 years old.

On December 18, 1912, Dawson formally unveiled Piltdown Man and declared it England's oldest human. Scientists and the public were abuzz. Even more exciting was the possibility that Piltdown Man was the missing link scientists had been looking for — proof that humans evolved over millions of years and shared an ancestor with apes, as suggested by Charles Darwin's theory.

Was Piltdown Man the Missing Link Between Apes and Humans?

Sir Arthur Smith Woodward was a man of science, and he was convinced that Piltdown Man was that link. Woodward believed that as early humans evolved from apes, their brains got bigger, and then they lost their big apelike jaws. (Other scientists thought the jaws were lost before the brains got bigger.) To Woodward, Piltdown Man seemed to be right in the middle. He had the big jaw of an ape and the big brain of a human. So Piltdown Man must be the missing link between ape and human. Some American and French paleontologists (people who study fossils) shook their heads in disagreement. The jaw was too big to be part of a human skull. And key fossil evidence was missing — the chin and the bony knob where the jaw fits into the skull. Without those bits, it was impossible to tell if the jaw belonged to the obviously human skull.

This is what people thought Piltdown Man might have looked like.

For the next couple of summers, Woodward dug off and on at the Piltdown site with Dawson. But it was Dawson who did most of the digging, and often he was alone at the site. Later digs uncovered a few more fossils and artifacts, including a carved elephant's thighbone.

Although there was disagreement among scientists, Piltdown Man clung to the human family tree for the next forty years. Then other fossils began turning up in China, Indonesia and Africa. These remains proved that scientists like Woodward had been wrong about the order of human development. They clearly showed that early humans had lost the big jaw first, then developed the big brain. There was something just not right about Piltdown Man. Fast-forward to 1953.

HUMAN FAMILY TREE

Charles Darwin forever altered ideas about where humans came from with his 1859 book *On the Origin of Species*. In the book, he explained how species change over time through a process called natural selection. He hinted that humans and apes probably shared a common ape-like ancestor.

Darwin's ideas created a sensation. People didn't like to think that humans were related to apes. Supporters and enemies quickly drew battle lines.

By the time Charles Dawson was digging for fossils at Piltdown, most scientists accepted Darwin's theory of evolution, and the race was on to find more evidence to support the natural selection process. That's why Piltdown Man was so exciting. He seemed to be proof of this process.

Today, high-tech science has traced the evolutionary path of humans more accurately. We evolved in Africa and became fully modern about 100 000 years ago. Questions will always swirl around the details of human evolution, but pulling off a hoax like Piltdown Man is much more difficult today than it was a century ago.

These are some of the primates on the primate family tree who share a common ancestor.

The Hoax Busters

On July 30, 1953, an anthropologist named Joseph Weiner stared at the skull of Piltdown Man, which was on display at London's Natural History Museum. He too felt there was something not quite right about the skull.

Weiner got talking to geologist Kenneth Oakley, who believed that Piltdown Man was a fake. Oakley had come across an old research paper describing how fluorine in water in the soil builds up in buried bones and teeth. He had measured the fluorine in the Piltdown remains. The test showed that Piltdown Man was, at most, 100 000 years old. Woodward had believed the remains were 500 000 years old.

Weiner and Oakley decided to team up and investigate further. They used a file to wear down some ape molars to see what they looked like. Hmm. Piltdown Man's "worn" molars and the filed-down ape molars had strikingly similar surface scratches. Then X-rays showed that one of the Piltdown teeth had just appeared before its owner died — it was way too new a tooth to be worn down as it was. Had the Piltdown teeth been tampered with?

OTHER SUSPECTS

Sir Arthur Conan Doyle, author of the Sherlock Holmes mysteries. He was a Piltdown Man supporter and visited the site frequently. Guilty? Not likely. Conan Doyle believed in far-out things, such as fairies. But believing in Piltdown was not that unusual at the time.

Martin Hinton, student. Hinton later became chief zoologist at the Natural History Museum. He hated Arthur Smith Woodward and may have wanted to embarrass him by faking some old bones. After Hinton's death, scientists found a trunk of his at the museum full of fake artifacts. Guilty? Possibly.

Pierre Teilhard de Chardin, priest, anthropologist and philosopher. He was the person who found the tooth that had been painted Vandyke brown. In letters, de Chardin suggested that a second Piltdown site was found in 1913, not 1915 as Dawson claimed. Did de Chardin bury the tooth for Dawson to find? Guilty? Possibly.

SIR ARTHUR CONAN DOYLE

MARTIN HINTON

PIERRE TEILHARD DE CHARDIN

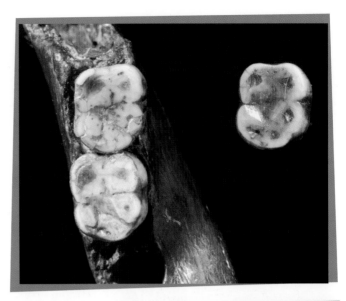

Piltdown Man's worn molars embedded in its apelike jaw

The scientists tried an improved fluorine test. It indicated that the skull could be from the last ice age (40 000 to 12 000 years ago). But the jaw and teeth were definitely not that old — in fact, they were much more modern.

Weiner and Oakley didn't stop there. They looked into the stains on the surface of the fossils. One tooth, it turned out, had been painted to look old with Vandyke brown, a popular color in the early 1900s. The pair drilled into the stained jawbone and uncovered the white color of new bone just under the surface. Drilling also produced bone shavings identical to the ones produced when fresh bone was drilled. This was no old skull, but rather one made to look old.

The scientists next tested the flints and animal bones that had been found at Piltdown. They had been artificially stained, too. Fakes! Weiner and Oakley also discovered that someone had used a steel knife to carve the elephant thighbone found at Piltdown. Steel is a modern invention. Piltdown and the objects found there were starting to look highly suspicious.

By 1959, a new dating method was available. It proved that Piltdown Man was less than 800 years old. And his jaw was even younger — by a few centuries!

The find of the century turned out to be the hoax of the century. But who was the hoaxer, and what was his motive?

Nabbed?

When you're looking for a hoaxer, start with the people closest to the hoax, in this case, the "discoverer" of the remains, Charles Dawson. He was always vague about when he first encountered the gravel pit and when the workers gave him the skull pieces. His own story of the discovery was different from Woodward's story.

It turned out that Charles Dawson had a long history of making things up. By age 12, he had an impressive fossil collection that had earned him the nickname the Wizard of Sussex. Everywhere he went, he found fossils. And most of his early discoveries were spectacular, such as another "missing link" that proved mammals had evolved from dinosaurs. (Now we know this is not true.)

Dawson's finds were spectacular, all right — spectacular hoaxes. Scientists found proof that most of them had been faked. Did he also fake Piltdown Man? Most likely, but the truth went to the grave with Dawson in 1915.

SKEPTIC'S TOOLBOX

As you read about Piltdown Man, were your hoax antennae twitching?

- Piltdown Man's discoverer, Charles Dawson, was the only witness when most of the discoveries were made.
- Dawson was always vague on when and how the fossils were found. No one ever knew for sure.
- Piltdown's champion, Sir Arthur Smith Woodward, was well known, respected and an expert, although not in physical anthropology.
- There was pride involved. Before Piltdown Man, the oldest human fossils were from France and Germany. If modern humans appeared first in England, well, it would be a sign of English superiority.

Gentleman Naturalist Gone Bad

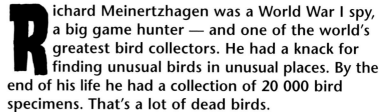

Richard Meinertzhagen was a World War I spy, a big game hunter — and one of the world's greatest bird collectors. He had a knack for finding unusual birds in unusual places. By the end of his life he had a collection of 20 000 bird specimens. That's a lot of dead birds.

In the late 1800s and early 1900s, ornithology (the study of birds) involved shooting birds and either stuffing them to look lifelike or creating "study skins." To make a study skin, the preparer removes the bird's organs, muscles and the bones in the torso and carefully sews the skin back together, leaving the feathers intact. Study skins allow scientists to compare characteristics of different bird species in detail.

Well-preserved skins last hundreds of years and are extremely valuable, especially today, when modern ornithologists shoot birds with cameras, not guns. Comparing photos or videos is more difficult than comparing specimens. Some study skins are especially valuable because they are of birds that are now endangered or even extinct.

Richard Meinertzhagen traveled the world, shooting birds and preparing skins. He wrote scientific papers and books, including the famous *Birds of Arabia*. His study skins are still used today by scientists — his collection was donated to the Natural History Museum in England.

Does it matter that Meinertzhagen was a liar and a thief?

A study skin

The Birdman

Born in 1878, Meinertzhagen grew up wealthy in a medieval English abbey. Surrounded by gardens, meadows and woods filled with wildlife, the country estate was tended by about 300 servants and tenants.

Meinertzhagen boasted that as a boy, he had perched on the knee of Charles Darwin, the famous scientist who set out the theory of evolution (see page 9). His diaries spoke of other famous scientists of the day who inspired his interest in the natural world. He strolled the countryside, gun in hand, developing a keen interest in birds.

Later, as a soldier in the British Army, when he wasn't busy shooting the enemy, he shot birds. Meinertzhagen was stationed in the Middle East and India and became the world's only authority on the location of fourteen bird species he had observed in India and Pakistan.

Meinertzhagen was a big name in the birding world. He donated his diaries, written from 1899 on, to Rhodes House at Oxford University in 1965. He died two years later.

Mottisfont Abbey, where Richard Meinertzhagen grew up

Foul Feathers

Twenty-five years after Meinertzhagen's death, ornithologist Pamela Rasmussen began writing a book about the birds of southern Asia. She inspected tens of thousands of study skins from American and British museums, including many collected by the famous Meinertzhagen. When you've examined that many skins, you can make a pretty good guess about who prepared a particular skin.

Most skin preparers have signature styles. To remove a bird's brain, for example, one collector might pull the brain out through a small hole in the back of the skull, while another might slice off the entire back of the skull. One person might use a wire, another a stick to support the bird's body.

X-rays revealed that the three birds in Meinertzhagen's collection (in the red boxes on the right) are identical to birds found in the collections of three other naturalists (on the left). Meinertzhagen claimed he shot the three birds in 1952 while visiting the Indian subcontinent.

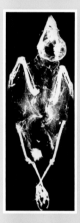 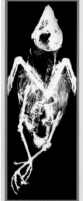

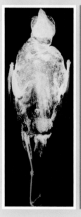 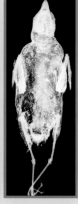

In the midst of her research, Rasmussen came across an alarming article in a bird journal, written by ornithologist Alan Knox. He wrote that Meinertzhagen had stolen study skins from the Natural History Museum and passed them off as his own. Knox gave several examples, including two redpoll bird skins Meinertzhagen claimed he had shot in France in 1953. These had actually been stolen from the collection of Richard Bowdler Sharpe, who had shot and stuffed the redpolls in England in 1884. Later, another scientist took X-rays that confirmed the redpoll skins had indeed been prepared by Sharpe in his signature style. Meinertzhagen had simply tied new tags with false information onto the birds' legs.

If there was one Meinertzhagen hoax, could there be more? Rasmussen wondered. She contacted colleagues, and they began to sift through Meinertzhagen's collection.

It took years of careful detective work. Rasmussen built up a database of X-rays so that she and her colleagues could compare skins and connect them to the people who had collected them. Rasmussen was surprised when X-rays of one collector's study skins showed that safety matches had been used to support them. It was a quirk she had never seen before. When a safety match popped up in one of Meinertzhagen's study skins, Rasmussen knew the specimen wasn't his. Missing skins from several museums were found in Meinertzhagen's collection.

Rasmussen believes that all the birds Meinertzhagen claimed to have collected in

Burma and Ceylon (now Sri Lanka) were actually stolen. About half the study skins from India were stolen, as were many from Afghanistan.

More detective work suggested that many of Meinertzhagen's early study skins had been pinched from other collections. The skins collected in his later years were more likely to be genuine. Scientists wonder if, as he got older, the gentleman naturalist wished he had collected more skins when he was a young man. Meinertzhagen may have decided to add specimens to his earlier collection by stealing them from museums.

DARWIN'S PIPE — UP IN SMOKE

What scientific society would pass up the chance to acquire a pipe owned by the father of evolutionary theory, Charles Darwin?

Famed birder, and documented liar, Richard Meinertzhagen donated Darwin's mahogany pipe to England's Linnean Society in 1958. You can still smell the tobacco, he assured society members. The pipe's stem was reportedly made from the tibia (part of the leg bone) of an albatross. The pipe was proudly displayed in the society's office.

Then one day, Pat Morris, a scientist and well-known taxidermist (someone who prepares dead animals for display), had a close look at the pipe. If that was the tibia of an albatross, the bird would be 2 m (6 ft. 5 in.) high, with spindly legs, he calculated. An albatross stands less than 1 m (3 ft.) high.

Marks stamped on the pipe revealed the truth — it was made in Birmingham, England, in 1928. Darwin died in 1882. Meinertzhagen strikes again!

The famous pipe

15

To Catch a Thief

The murky world of Meinertzhagen was further revealed by examining his diaries, travel schedules, bird labels and old letters.

These documents showed that some people knew about the fakery during Meinertzhagen's lifetime. In one letter, an ornithologist who had gone on safari with Meinertzhagen accused him of swiping skins from museums in Paris, Leningrad and New York. Another ornithologist wrote that Meinertzhagen's bird collection was so flawed it should be burned. Gossip about Meinertzhagen was plentiful. Birding pals commented among themselves that their collections got a little lighter after a visit from Meinertzhagen.

The Natural History Museum in London, however, was the gentleman naturalist's main target. Meinertzhagen was a regular at the museum's bird room. He often visited at lunchtime, when only one staff member was on duty. One curator reported that he handed Meinertzhagen a box with eight bird specimens. It was returned with only seven.

THE HOAX THAT WASN'T

Picture a cat-sized mole with a duck's bill. It sounds made up. But this furry creature, which also had webbed feet and a tail like a beaver, had European scientists all hot and bothered for a good ninety years.

In 1799, when George Shaw at England's Natural History Museum was sent a dried specimen of the strange-looking creature from Australia, he thought it was a fake. Explorers were sending all sorts of strange animals and plants back to Europe from far-flung places. And Shaw knew that clever Chinese and Japanese taxidermists had fooled many by stitching the head and trunk of monkeys to the hind parts of fish.

But peeling apart the specimen revealed a real animal, not a hoax. Shaw described the animal, a platypus, in his book *The Naturalist's Miscellany*. British scientist Everard Home spent years teasing out the platypus's secrets. He thought that platypups (an informal name for baby platypuses) formed and hatched from eggs while inside the mother.

Scientists spent almost the entire nineteenth century arguing over where the platypus belonged in the animal kingdom. Was it a mammal or some kind of furred reptile or a bird? It wasn't until forty years after the creature was first identified that a French naturalist actually witnessed platypups nursing — just like mammals. Finally, after another forty years, the mystery was definitively solved when a naturalist shot a platypus that had just laid a soft, leathery egg and was about to lay another.

Scientists had their answer: the platypus was an egg-laying mammal that nursed its young.

But there was another mystery. What about the duck-like bill? It took another 100 years to solve that one. The bill works like a short-range radar system. A row of nerves picks up electrical signals from dinner — insects and crustaceans lurking in the murky mud bottoms of streams and lakes.

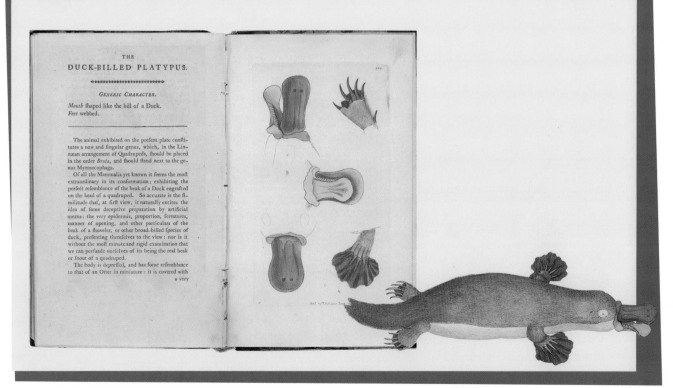

BIRD FRAUD AND THE MISSING LINK TO DINOSAURS

Nothing excites dinosaur hunters more than a fossil that screams, "Yes, I'm evidence that birds evolved from dinosaurs!" So in 1999, when a fossil with the tail of a dinosaur and the upper body of a bird was discovered, it was exciting times in the world of paleontology.

Named Archaeoraptor, the fossil strengthened the dino/bird theory. It came from China's Liaoning province, an area known for authentic, and sometimes extraordinary, dinosaur and bird finds.

Well, it was extraordinary, all right. The fossilized skeleton was made from two species that had been glued together. No one knows who did the gluing or why.

We do know that the skeleton was smuggled to the United States and auctioned off for $80 000 to a dinosaur museum in Utah. A few months later, the fraud was revealed when Chinese scientists bought a fossil that turned out to be the other half of one part of the skeleton.

The fossil *was* a hoax, but there was a silver lining. Archaeoraptor's tail and hind limbs were later found to be a new kind of birdlike, feathered dinosaur called Microraptor. It is the smallest adult dinosaur ever found. The rest of the fossil was identified as a fish-eating ancient bird that lived about 110 million years ago, the first of its kind to be discovered.

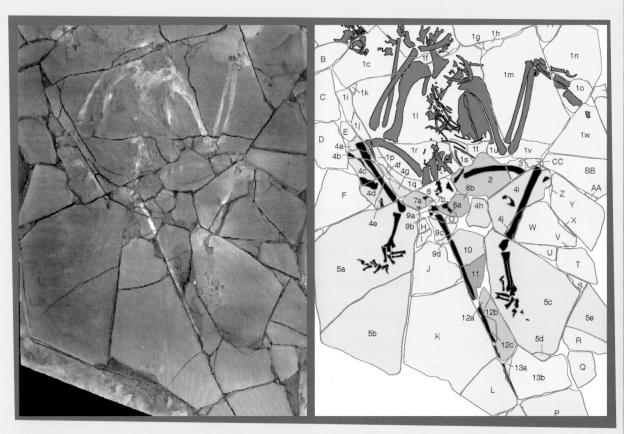

A CT scan of Archaeoraptor revealed the truth: two fossils glued together. The bright red shows the remains of an ancient bird. The black bones belong to the smallest adult dinosaur ever found.

In fact, as far back as 1919, Meinertzhagen had been banned from the museum after he tried to walk out with nine study skins. He was allowed back a year and a half later. However, the naturalist continued to cause trouble. Scotland Yard was called in after valuable journals on bird parasites went missing. Even though it was clear Meinertzhagen had stolen them, he was not arrested or otherwise punished. How did he get away with it? Only a few people knew about the thefts. And Meinertzhagen was rich, with friends in high places and a big bird collection to donate. The museum was counting on getting its birds back, plus more.

What no one foresaw was the extent of Meinertzhagen's trickery. He had not only stolen specimens but had reported seeing species in places they'd never been seen before. He also recorded sightings of rare or possibly extinct birds. These thefts and lies misled scientists who were trying to get an accurate picture of bird populations. But exposing the elaborate hoax was only possible when Knox, Rasmussen and their colleagues started ruffling some feathers.

Before we leave Meinertzhagen, let's take another look at that story he told of sitting on Charles Darwin's knee. Meinertzhagen was barely four when Darwin died, and ill health had plagued Darwin during the last few years of his life. He rarely left home. In addition, there was no mention of the Meinertzhagen family in any of Darwin's letters. The story, it appears, may be just another dead end in Meinertzhagen's amazing maze of lies.

When a Hoax Is Not a Hoax

The Philippines is circled in red.

In 1971, journalists announced a startling discovery. Deep in the Philippine rain forest, a tribe had been found living as if they were back in the Stone Age. They wore leaves and used stone axes. They gathered food rather than growing it. They slept in caves. Their lives were simple and basic, and they didn't fight! Conflicts were settled gently, with compromise. They were the Tasaday, and they were about to become a worldwide sensation.

A rain forest like this one was home to an unknown people.

Half a world away, freeways were jammed with traffic, factories pumped out everything from hula hoops to lava lamps, the United States and the Soviet Union (now Russia) had nuclear weapons pointed at each another. Some young people called hippies refused to buy into this hectic world. They wanted to drop out of the rat race, and they were declaring that all the world needed was love, love, love.

The Tasaday were the opposite of everything that was wrong with modern culture. They were like Stone Age hippies.

The Lost Tribe

Who found the lost tribe? A rich former playboy named Manuel Elizalde, Jr. Throughout the 1960s, Elizalde had worked to protect and help various tribes of the Philippines. He brought them medicine, food, tools and even weapons.

One day, a T'boli hunter named Dafal told Elizalde about a wild people living in the rain forest. Did he want to meet them? Of course! Elizalde helicoptered into a clearing in the forest to meet three Tasaday men and two boys, who trembled and fainted at the sight of the huge metal bird. Elizalde eased their fears with gifts of bead necklaces. Soon he had met most of the twenty-six Tasadays.

Tasaday people inspect a helicopter.

Elizalde brought in the press. Reporters from *National Geographic*, *Reader's Digest* and Associated Press and a television crew from NBC broke the story to the world.

"Lost Tribe Found in Cotabato," trumpeted the headlines. (Cotabato is a province in the southern Philippines.) But the story really got rolling when *National Geographic* ran an article called "First Glimpse of a Stone Age Tribe" with photos of leaf-wearing, vine-swinging natives. Readers were told the Tasaday had no words for "agriculture" or "war," and there seemed to be nothing a big hug wouldn't cure. For people living a fast-paced lifestyle, reading about the slow-paced Tasaday was like finding out that paradise really existed. People couldn't get enough of the peaceable Tasaday.

Anthropologists wanted to study the Tasaday. Two of them, American Frank Lynch and Filipino Carlos Fernandez, published the first scholarly report on the Tasaday. It called the Tasaday an important group that shed light on how humans lived thousands of years ago.

GOD'S HAND — A FRAUD

"The devil made me do it." That's what Shinichi Fujimura said after he was caught red-handed planting fake artifacts at an archaeological site in Japan. (Archaeology is the study of past human cultures.)

Fujimura was good at faking — so good that people nicknamed him God's Hand for his supernatural luck. So good that for more than twenty years he fooled everyone — including scientists digging right next to him. Fujimura would plant artifacts at a site while no one was looking, then dig them up, claiming he had found them. The artifacts were real stone tools taken from other archaeological sites.

It was only in October 2000 that skeptical journalists — at the urging of a skeptical scientist — followed the amateur archaeologist to a dig 350 km (217 mi.) northeast of Tokyo. There they filmed Fujimura planting some stone tools.

The moral of the story: if something seems too good to be true, it probably is.

Later, Fernandez returned with another Filipino anthropologist, David Baradas. The pair spoke at least eight Philippine dialects between them and quickly picked up some of the Tasaday language. As they began to communicate with the Tasaday, it became clear that the "Stone Age tribe" was not quite what it seemed.

Yes, the Tasaday hunted and collected fruit and roots from the rain forest as Stone Age hunter-gatherers had, but Elizalde's men were also giving them rice. Baradas also noticed that although the Tasaday had no word for "war," they quickly picked up weapons when strangers were spotted nearby. The anthropologists came to see that the Tasaday were not "cave people" — they just wanted to please Elizalde and receive his gifts.

Then, without warning, an armed raid interrupted the scientists' research. Gunmen exchanged fire with Elizalde's men. Frightened, the two anthropologists flew out of the forest on the first helicopter.

Did Elizalde stage the raid to get rid of the anthropologists? wondered Baradas. He had noticed that whenever scientists were around, Elizalde's men were watching. Elizalde was suspicious of the scientists, too. He believed they only wanted fame and did not care about the Tasaday. Elizalde limited the scientists' access to the group. As a result, most day-to-day information about the tribe came from journalists, not scientists.

In 1972, Elizalde convinced Philippine dictator Ferdinand Marcos to declare 19 000 ha (46 950 acres) of land a protected reserve for the Tasaday and their neighbors, the Manobo Blit. Outsiders were forbidden to log, mine or exploit the reserve in any way. Four years later, the reserve was made off-limits to scientists and journalists. They were threatened with prison if they set foot on Tasaday land. Was Elizalde protecting the Tasaday, or was he trying to preserve their land for himself for some future use? The Elizalde family businesses included mining, and rumors of gold were circulating.

This 1972 photo shows the Tasaday sitting around a fire.

The Elusive Truth

Swiss journalist Oswald Iten was in the Philippines in 1986 when dictator Marcos was toppled from power and fled. Elizalde had already left, having moved to Costa Rica three years earlier, reportedly with millions of dollars.

A Tasaday child named Lobo holds a pet bird on a vine thread leash.

While talking to a local priest, Iten was told that the Tasaday story was a hoax. Iten decided to find out the truth and offered an exposé of the hoax to *National Geographic*. He figured they would want to set the record straight. He was wrong, but that didn't stop him.

By this time, the area where the Tasaday lived had become chaotic and dangerous. People had guns, and there was little government control. Iten managed to sneak into the Tasaday area with a Filipino reporter and a tribal chief as interpreters. They met some Tasaday, dressed not in leaves but in tattered T-shirts and jeans.

Communicating through the translators, the Tasaday told Iten they were actually T'boli and Manobo tribal farmers. Elizalde, they said, had given them gifts in exchange for acting like cave people. And by the way, where was the helicopter they had been promised?

Iten's story broke in a Swiss newspaper. Then an American news program broadcast "The Tribe That Never Was." Almost overnight the Tasaday were labeled fakes and the greatest hoax since Piltdown Man. Anthropologists everywhere condemned the fraud. But was this hoax version of the story accurate?

The Real Story?

Twenty years later, the American Anthropology Association put the Tasaday "hoax" under a microscope. Their conclusions? The Tasaday were not a Stone Age people. Instead, they were most likely a group that at some point had become isolated from other tribes in the area. By studying the Tasaday language, linguists found the Tasaday spoke a dialect of Manobo. The split from other Manobo speakers probably happened no more than 200 years ago. Analyzing the dialect revealed that the Tasaday probably drifted from a group living 65 km (40 mi.) north.

Stories told by the Tasaday supported this account. The stories said their ancestors fled that area long ago when a terrible wind called "fugu" began killing everyone. Scientists believe the fugu was an epidemic, perhaps cholera, smallpox or measles. A small group — who became known as the Tasaday — found refuge in the rain forest and stayed. Believing they were the only survivors, they never traveled north where the killing wind might get them. They were cut off from the rest of the world when Elizalde discovered them.

So, a hoax? No. Hype? Yes. It was the media, not the scientists, who came up with the label Stone Age people. Stories like that sell magazines and newspapers.

The public accepted the story because when life is crazy-busy, it's nice to think that paradise still exists. And at a time when nuclear war threatened much of the world, it was even nicer to think that peace reigned in the rain forests of the Philippines. People in the 1970s wanted to believe what they read about the Tasaday because they envied their simple and peaceful life.

Who Won?

If the Tasaday story was a hoax, who had benefited from it? Not Elizalde. He was back in the Philippines, but he wasn't involved with mining and logging. And not the Tasaday. They were just as poor as they had been before they'd been "discovered," and losing their land to logging and mining would make them even poorer.

What about the scientists and journalists? Did they benefit? Some may have. Some journalists landed big stories. Some scientists gained attention. But other scientists and journalists had built their reputations on the Tasaday and looked bad when the "Stone Age tribe" was debunked. In the end, there were no big winners.

URBAN LEGEND

Urban legends are stories that claim to be true but aren't. They get passed from person to person and have something in common with hoaxes. As with hoaxes, the origins of an urban legend are fuzzy. The source is often a friend of a friend (or your sister's friend's mother or your granddad's barber), which makes it seem true.

One famous urban legend goes like this. A woman orders a chocolate chip cookie at a café in a well-known department store. She likes it so much she asks for the recipe. "Sure," says the waitress. "But it will cost you two-fifty." Later, the woman's credit card bill shows she had been charged not $2.50 but $250! In revenge, she e-mails the recipe free to everyone she knows and asks them to pass it on.

It turns out the "pricey cookie" urban legend has been around for a long time — about fifty years, in fact. Back then, the recipe only cost $25, got sent around by snail mail and involved a different department store.

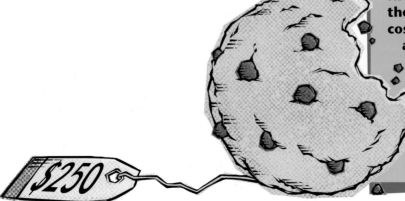

Doug and Dave's Circular Adventure

Doug Bower had to come clean. His wife noticed how much mileage he was racking up on their car. Why such long distances?

It turns out this World War II veteran was hanging out a lot with a buddy, another veteran named Dave Chorley. The pals were traveling all over their little corner of England, flattening crops into circles.

The pair began making crop circles in the 1970s, about the same time the New Age movement was taking off. New Agers believed in everything from the healing power of crystals and the existence of spirits (from angels to aliens) to the cosmic energy of certain places.

Crop circles fit right in and soon started a whole new field of "scientific" research called cerealogy.

Who Dunnit?

While Doug and Dave secretly wound their way across the English countryside with circle-making tools (planks, wires and rope), three groups surfaced to explain the phenomenon: people who truly believed the circles had some sort of mystical origin, people who knew how to make a buck or two and scientists who were genuinely intrigued.

One weather scientist was particularly interested, especially when he came across an explanation for such circles put forward in 1880, almost 100 years before Doug and Dave got to work. Back then a scientist named Rand Capron had come across a circle in a field in southern England. He described

Dave Chorley (left) and Doug Bower (right) began making crop circles in the 1970s, for fun.

some standing stalks at the center, flattened stalks around them and a wall of untouched stalks ringing the area. Violent storms had hit the area not long before, and Capron theorized that "cyclonic wind action" was the cause.

Could there be a natural cause for crop circles? Capron's paper, along with some additional historical accounts, persuaded another weather scientist, Terence Meaden, to investigate further. Other scientists couldn't resist the mystery either.

While the scientists plugged away at theories, Doug and Dave got more creative. Big circles, little circles, rectangles — all sorts of shapes were cropping up in farmers' fields throughout the 1980s. In fact, there were so many circles that there's no way the duo could have made them all. Oh, Doug and Dave were fast — they could tamp down a 12 m (40 ft.) circle in fifteen minutes — but not fast enough to cover the entire English countryside with crop circles. Obviously, Doug and Dave's whirlwind tour was inspiring others.

The pranks also spawned a whole new group of circle believers called croppies. Some croppies believed UFOs landing in fields made the circles. Some even thought the circles might be elaborate messages from extraterrestrials. Others believed the English countryside was brimming over with electromagnetic energy, as were select fields elsewhere around the globe where crop circles also popped up.

Two British artists launched a collective called Circlemakers and turned crop circles into an art form. One of them, artist John Lundberg, visited the Canadian west coast in August 2007 to create circles for the environmental organization Greenpeace.

In 1990, the most elaborate and beautiful shapes appeared. That same year, a huge gathering of croppies from around the world was held in Somerset, England. The Glastonbury Symposium was the place to be if you wanted to check out a crop circle with fellow believers.

Not to be outdone, Terence Meaden formed the Circles Effect Research Organization. Research focused on electrically charged whirlwinds. The government even mulled over the idea of funding crop circle research.

Then, in 1991, Doug and Dave confessed. The joke, they felt, had gone far enough. But diehard croppies wouldn't give up. The circles were real, they insisted — it was Doug and Dave who were the frauds.

Copycats and Cash Crops

Many people had a lot invested in crop circles. Some had written books. Some gave tours for which they charged hundreds of dollars. The Glastonbury Symposium was becoming a big event. And true croppies didn't want to stop believing that crop circles were mystical places with mystical origins. After all, southern England, which is crop circle central, is home to Stonehenge and other ancient sites and burial grounds. Croppies held to their belief that mysterious forces in the area were responsible for the circles. Sure, Doug and Dave could have made some of the circles, croppies acknowledged, but what about all the ones they couldn't have made? And what about Capron's paper from the 1880s?

Non-croppies countered with other theories. Hoaxers have been at work all through history, they said. Capron's crop circle could easily have been the work of someone having a little fun at a farmer's expense. Plus people are copycats. When newspapers and magazines printed more and more circle stories between 1981 and 1987, the number of crop circles rose, too.

Scientist and writer Matt Ridley decided to prove that anyone could make a crop circle by creating a couple himself and fooling crop circle "experts." At first, he tried a garden roller, then switched to Doug and Dave's plank method. Traipsing around a wheat field in July without leaving a trail was fairly easy, Ridley discovered. Some circle-makers he met used two bar stools, hopping from one to the other to avoid leaving footprints.

Ridley wrote about his adventures. The reaction? Fraud, cried the croppies. They even accused him of being a spy, part of a government plot to keep the real story a secret.

A New Old Theory

So who or what is responsible for crop circles? Are they all pranks, or do some have natural, or even supernatural, origins?

A very few scientists still think southern England is susceptible to circle-making geomagnetic whirlwinds. Jeremy Northcote, an Australian researcher, decided to test this theory. He used computer software to map the distribution of crop circles reported in England in 2002. If crop circles were caused by some kind of natural phenomenon, such as whirlwinds, the circles would be scattered randomly, he reasoned. Yet he found that the circles were nearly always close to highly populated areas, main roads or cultural sites, such as Stonehenge.

Northcote concluded that the circles were not made by whirlwinds. Instead, the data suggested that the circles were deliberately created to attract attention.

Scientists now generally accept that crop circles are human made and consider more research a waste of time. Croppies, however, continue to search for a nonhuman answer. The truth is out there … somewhere.

GOING AROUND IN CIRCLES

Botanist Gretel van Rooyen investigates strange circles on the sandy plains of the southern African country of Namibia. A typical circle has tall, lush grasses surrounding a bare center and measures 3 to 10 m (10 to 30 ft.) across.

Could the cause be a fungus, as in fairy rings (see page 28)? In 1978, researchers decided to find out. They measured the circles. If fungus was the cause, they theorized, the circles would get bigger as the fungus grew. After twenty-two years, researchers went back to check. The circles were no bigger, so they concluded that fungus was an unlikely culprit.

Termites were another possibility. Maybe termites were carrying off seeds, so that no plants grew. But Dr. van Rooyen and her team dug trenches up to 2 m (6 ft.) deep inside the circles, and there was not a termite in sight.

Then Dr. van Rooyen checked for radioactivity in the soil. Negative. Okay, maybe it was the milkbush plants that grew in the area. They are poisonous.

Do they leave toxic debris in the soil that stops grass from growing? Dr. van Rooyen took soil from under milkbushes and found that grasses grew just fine in it. Growing grass in soil taken from the barren middle of a circle, however, was impossible.

The verdict? Well, Dr. van Rooyen hasn't given up on science, but at this point in her research, the Namibian rings are still a mystery.

A BEGINNER'S GUIDE TO MAKING CROP CIRCLES

1. Drill a hole on each end of a short plank. Tie on a rope. This is your grass flattener.

2. Tiptoe out into a grassy field with your grass flattener. Plant a stake in the ground and tie a long rope to it.

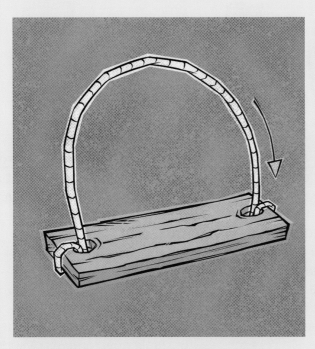

3. Use the stake and rope like a big compass to tromp a circle in the grass.

4. Use the grass flattener to stamp down all the grass inside the circle. Congratulations! You're a crop circle maker!

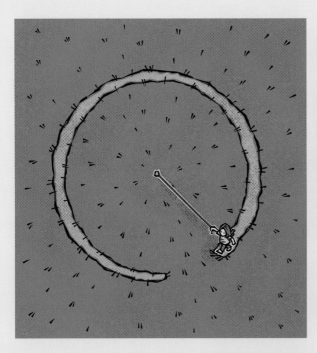

Star in a Jar

Garbage! Fraud! Scientific schlock! Those were the words used to describe an experiment done by two scientists back in 1989. The experiment was on cold fusion, a process that promised humanity cheap, clean fuel forever. Sound too good to be true?

Sure, but a lot of people wanted an alternative to oil. Oil, used to fuel cars, power plants, trains, ships — you name it — runs the modern world. But oil has its problems. For one thing, it's nonrenewable — once the world runs out, that's it. And some of the world's current supply of oil is in countries with unstable governments. A sudden change in government might shut off the supply. Finally, burning oil pumps carbon dioxide into Earth's atmosphere, raising Earth's average temperature. There had to be a better alternative, and cold fusion looked awfully attractive.

Anyone who could make cold fusion work would be a hero.

Cars, homes and industries gobble up huge amounts of energy.

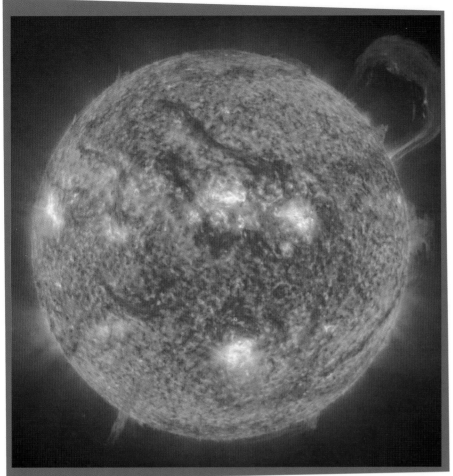

Deep in the sun's core, fusion creates hydrogen and bursts of energy.

Jam Jar of Dreams

Fusion is what happens in the sun's core. There atoms behave in a way you never see them behaving on Earth. Extreme heat and pressure in the core allows protons in the nuclei of atoms to get really close together, something they hate to do here on Earth. Here they're like the north poles of two magnets — they push each other away. But in the sun's core, the nuclei in deuterium atoms (deuterium is heavy hydrogen) unavoidably meet — okay, they're rammed together — creating helium and a huge burst of energy. That burst of energy is what interests scientists. They hope to harness it to produce power.

Scientists have tried to mimic the process that happens inside the sun. It's called hot fusion, and it's how a hydrogen bomb works. Some scientists are looking at hot fusion as a peaceful means of solving Earth's energy crisis, and several countries are working together to build a hot fusion reactor in France. But it takes lots of energy to create hot fusion, it costs billions of dollars, and there's no guarantee it will work on a large scale as an energy source.

In contrast, cold fusion would tap nuclear energy at room temperature. And more importantly, it would be cheap to do. It's like a star in a jar.

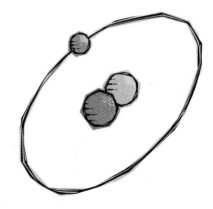

Deuterium atom

Energy Magic

Scientists scoff at the idea of cold fusion. It goes against a fundamental rule of physics — that energy cannot be created or destroyed but only changed from one form to another. But chemists Stanley Pons and Martin Fleischmann set out to prove that nuclear fusion without the high temperatures and pressure of the sun was possible. They were intrigued by the thought of a cheap, clean power source. They worked in secret for five years, spending $100 000 of their own money on their experiments.

In 1989, the pair unleashed a firestorm of excitement — and controversy — when they announced that they had made cold fusion work. Not only did their method work, they said, it was easy.

Pons and Fleischmann used an insulated glass jar containing heavy water. (Heavy water has deuterium atoms.) Two electrodes — one made of platinum and the other of palladium (a precious metal) — were placed in heavy water. The electrodes created a low voltage electric current (high voltage would produce high heat), which drove the deuterium into the palladium. The scientists said this process fused the nuclei of the deuterium atoms and generated heat for hours.

The Pons and Fleischmann experiment suggested that a little bit of energy could produce a lot of energy through cold fusion, even though the rules of physics say that's impossible. And, amazingly, the deuterium that made it all seem possible is available in ordinary sea water. In fact, just 5 mL (1 tsp.) of water has enough deuterium to produce as much energy as a gallon of gasoline. Cold fusion would be an energy bonanza.

Was it fraud, faulty science or the real thing?

Martin Fleischmann (left) and Stanley Pons (right) created a lot of controversy when they announced that their cold fusion experiment worked.

Fusion Confusion

Whatever it was, it led to a rush of experiments. That's what scientists do: they experiment and publish their findings in a scientific journal. Then other scientists repeat the experiment. If enough scientists get the same result, it's probably a new discovery. If not, it's back to the drawing board.

In the case of cold fusion, things didn't quite work out that way. Pons and Fleischmann submitted a paper explaining their method to a scientific journal, and it was accepted. But the story hit the newspapers, radio and television before the paper was published. The media went crazy. A new energy source was big news that could change the world.

But there was a complication. While Pons and Fleischmann were waiting for a patent on their fusion process, they refused to tell other scientists exactly how it worked. And to make matters worse, Pons joked that the process was so easy, he was going to let his school-age son try it.

Criticism rolled in. Pons and Fleischmann responded by faxing a draft paper about cold fusion to scientists around the world. Researchers at universities in Hungary, Texas and Georgia were the first to report back. Yes! Cold fusion worked for them, too, using the Fleischmann-Pons technique. The duo were treated like rock stars. Pons had to get an unlisted phone number.

The Hungarian experiment, however, was never confirmed. In Texas, researchers found that an electrical problem had given false results. And in Georgia, scientists figured out, days after their attempt, that they had also gotten false readings from equipment. Then the respected Massachusetts Institute of Technology tried it. The experiment failed.

NOT A GAS, A GIMMICK

Ever since the car became popular 100 years ago, hoaxers have claimed it's possible to make gas out of water.

As early as 1917, hoaxer John Andrews convinced the U.S. Navy that a little pill, plopped into a tank full of water, could turn the water into gasoline. It never worked.

In 1954, Guido Franch made the same claim. To convince fools, uh, people, to fork over $1000, Franch would dump a mysterious green powder into a bucket of water, mix it up and pour it into a lawn mower. Vroom! The mower would start running on mota (that's "atom" spelled backward) fuel.

Not so fast. The green powder was ordinary vegetable dye. Franch had played a simple con game. The mower was running on good ol' gas.

The free energy hoax continues.

It wasn't long before the scientific community was howling "Hoax!" The search for cold fusion fizzled and died. One important supporter of fusion research, the U.S. Department of Energy, said cold fusion was a fantasy. They decided, instead, to continue pumping money into hot fusion. Pons left the United States to live and work in France. Fleischmann also left, eventually resettling in England.

Fusion Fever

The beauty of cold fusion — and its main problem — is that it promises so much for so little. Pons and Fleischmann, honest scientists, were caught up in a powerful dream of cheap power. Today, twenty years later, their experiment looks less like a hoax and more like wishful thinking. Bottom line: other scientists could not get the two scientists' experiment to work.

After Pons and Fleischmann's big announcement, some researchers continued to tinker with cold fusion experiments that *did* follow the rules of physics. In 2005, researchers announced success using a crystal discovered by the ancient Greeks 2000 years ago: lithium tantalate. The crystal is pyroelectric — when heated or cooled, it can generate a strong electrical field. Scientists at the University of California in Los Angeles put the crystal in a cylinder full of deuterium gas. Then they cooled it to –33°C (–27°F) and heated it to 7°C (45°F) within three and a half minutes. Some deuterium atoms fused and produced energy. But the device, about the size of a breadbox, used up more energy than it produced. It will never be useful for generating lots of power.

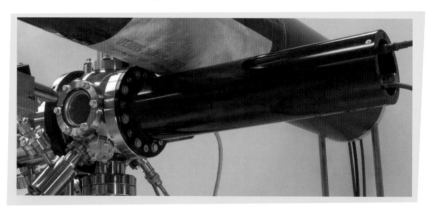

This breadbox-sized nuclear fusion device uses more power than it generates.

Still, some scientists remain hopeful about cold fusion. Who wouldn't be? As one scientist pointed out, 5 percent of the deuterium in the ocean could power the world for a million years. And if there's one thing that separates humans from the rest of Earth's animals, it's that four-letter word: hope. Sometimes, unfortunately, it gets in the way of good science.

PAPP GOES THE WEASEL

Imagine yourself back in the summer of 1966. Josef Papp is fished out of a rubber raft floating in the Atlantic off Brest, France. He's covered in blood.

Papp, a Hungarian-Canadian, says he has crossed the Atlantic in a homemade submarine in just thirteen hours. Afraid that the Russians would seize the sub, Papp sank it, barely escaping with his life. Think about it. At its shortest, the distance from Canada to France is still about 3500 km (2200 mi.)

How did Papp's submarine travel so far so fast? Cold fusion, of course. Or at least that's what he claimed.

Because the sub had sunk, there was no way to inspect it. But that wasn't all. A man using Papp's passport and looking like Papp had hopped a plane from Montreal to Paris not long before. Oh yeah, and inside Papp's pocket was a Paris-to-Brest train ticket. Hmm ... was Papp a weasel, a crank or a misunderstood genius? What do you think?

STORY 1

STORY 2

37

The Roswell Riddle

In mid-June 1947, rancher Mac Brazel found some debris — sticks, paper, aluminum foil, rubber, tape — spread across a patch of land on his New Mexico ranch. He was puzzled. What was this stuff?

Meanwhile, on June 24, pilot Kenneth Arnold was flying around Mount Rainier in Washington State looking for a crashed military aircraft. Instead he saw nine bright, disk-shaped objects flying in a chainlike formation, fast. Arnold calculated their speed at 2735 km/h (1700 m.p.h.). He'd never seen any flying objects like them. Arnold was no wingnut — he was an experienced pilot and a well-regarded salesman of fire-control equipment. He was believable. Yet to this day, no one knows for certain what he saw.

Newspapers and radio broadcasters got hold of the story, and away it went. For the next couple of weeks, sensational eyewitness accounts of flying saucers were reported all over North America. In total, there were more than 800 sightings, including eighteen in Canada. Even China had a saucer sighting.

Back in New Mexico, Mac Brazel started to wonder. Could the debris he had found be from a crashed flying saucer?

Examining the debris

Science and Fiction

On July 6, Brazel decided to alert the sheriff in nearby Roswell. The sheriff contacted the Roswell Army Air Field. The military picked up the debris. Two days later, an army officer dropped off a press release at the *Roswell Daily Record*, the local paper. The report said the debris was from something called a flying disk. The next day, the newspaper gave the story a more sensational twist. "RAAF Captures Flying Saucer on Ranch in Roswell Region," the headline screamed.

Newspapers across North America picked up the story. Another saucer sighting! The debris was shipped to an army base in Fort Worth, Texas. Officials there said it was part of a weather balloon used to track high-altitude wind direction and speed. Reporters were invited to see the debris and take pictures.

The first newspaper report

The July 9 newspaper headline in the *Fort Worth Star-Telegram* read, "'Disk-overy' Near Roswell Identified as Weather Balloon ..." Case closed.

Except that weather balloons don't carry wood strips attached to foil-coated parchmentlike paper or tape with markings on it. There were only two possibilities: it was a new-fangled weather balloon, or the government was covering up some new military technology that would make other countries nervous, particularly the Soviet Union (now known as Russia).

THE MEDIA AND THE MESSAGE

A news announcer states that a flying saucer has been spotted over the CN Tower, gives a few details and moves on to another story. Do you believe it? Probably. It's the news, after all.

For twenty years, Purdue University researcher Glenn Sparks studied how the media influences people's beliefs in the paranormal — ghosts, aliens and UFOs, for example. His research shows that news reports of a UFO sighting increase an audience's belief in UFOs.

If the reports demonstrate how technology can be used to fool people, belief tends to decrease.

Dr. Sparks has also noted that the more education people have, the less likely they are to believe in the paranormal. And people who watch TV shows about the paranormal are more likely to believe in it. Of course, it could be the other way around: believers in the paranormal are drawn to such shows.

That was a real possibility. Americans were terrified that the Russians were developing nuclear weapons. And the Russians were equally suspicious of the Americans. The two countries spent a lot of time and money spying on each other.

In fact, the military theory proved to be correct. The debris was from a balloon, but not a weather balloon. It was a specially designed, high-altitude balloon that was part of Project MOGUL, an effort to figure out if the Russians had nuclear weapons.

Maurice Ewing, a geophysicist (a scientist who uses physics to study Earth) at Columbia University, came up with the idea. He had made his mark by identifying the deep sound channel in the ocean. This is a layer 1.2 km (3/4 mi.) deep where sound can speed along for thousands of kilometers before fading away. The U.S. military used this deep-sea channel to listen for Soviet submarines.

Ewing was fairly certain that Earth's upper atmosphere had the same type of channel, because other scientists had already theorized that the Krakatau volcano explosion of 1883 was heard around the world through such a channel. If the Soviets were exploding nuclear weapons in the atmosphere, the explosions should be detectable, Ewing reasoned.

By 1946, research had started. Project MOGUL was top secret. If the Soviets found out about it, they would look for another way to test any nuclear weapons.

Spies?

This balloon was the Roswell UFO.

41

Up, Up and Away

Helium-filled balloons carried Project MOGUL's spy microphones into the air. (Balloons were used because they're quieter than airplanes.)

June 4, 1947, was the day that Project MOGUL flight number 4 was launched from Alamogordo, New Mexico. Twenty-three balloons took off, linked together in a chain 180 m (600 ft.) long and equipped with listening instruments. They were tracked to within 27 km (17 mi.) of Mac Brazel's ranch before disappearing.

Weather balloons often burst when the sun degrades the material. In this case, some of Project MOGUL's balloons may have popped, but the remaining ones probably floated on, gradually losing height and getting snagged in a tree. The microphones, batteries and other equipment were probably ripped off when the balloons first touched down. Lightened a bit, the balloons would have coasted along on the breeze a little farther. By the time the balloon chain crashed, the debris would be strewn over a wide area. This is what Brazel found.

Project MOGUL researchers had flown back to New York in early July before the flying saucer report appeared in the Roswell paper. They didn't associate the Roswell incident with the

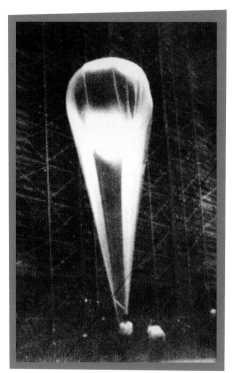

The Project MOGUL balloon is prepped for a flight.

THE LOCH NESS MYSTERY

Every now and then over the past 800 years, Scotland's Loch Ness monster pops up and startles some unsuspecting passerby. So pick a Nessie hoax, any hoax — a filmed Nessie, a photographed Nessie or how about a fossilized Nessie?

In 2003, Gerald McSorley was walking around Loch Ness when he stumbled over a fossil. Was it Nessie? The fossil was turned over to the National Museum of Scotland, where a paleontologist took a close look. The fossilized neck bones were embedded in limestone, a kind of rock not found in Loch Ness. And the fossil showed signs of being immersed in saltwater, not freshwater. Plus Loch Ness was formed about 15 000 years ago, while the fossil, of a marine plesiosaur, was about 155 million years old.

The fossil wasn't Nessie. It was probably planted there by a hoaxer. Still, Nessie lives on, if not in the lake, at least in people's imaginations.

missing balloons until years later. In 1994, the U.S. Air Force finally released information about Project MOGUL in *The Roswell Report: Fact Versus Fiction in the New Mexico Desert.*

At least, that's the official version. Some people still believe that an alien spacecraft landed at Roswell. After all, tourists love aliens, and tourists bring a lot of money into a town. So the myth of alien visitations gave Roswell some economic success. But was Project MOGUL a technological success? Sort of. While it failed to detect Soviet nuclear testing, it managed to record sound signals from rocket tests conducted in the upper atmosphere. And, it did give Roswell its "aliens."

Roswell, New Mexico, goes all out for aliens.

BIGFOOT BOB

A huge apelike creature walks away from the camera, then pauses. With a twist of his torso, he glances back. Bigfoot knows he's being filmed. Of course he does — he's Bob in a gorilla suit.

In 1967, Roger Patterson happened to have a film camera with him while horseback riding with a friend in Bluff Creek, California. A sudden movement of a big hairy creature startled one of the horses. Patterson grabbed his camera, catching Bigfoot in action. That's the story Patterson wanted everyone to believe, anyway. His film was actually faked.

Forty years later, journalists investigating Patterson and the film came up with the truth. Bob Heironimus confessed to wearing the suit for Patterson in exchange for $1000. Bob had told some close friends and later his wife.

The suit came from Philip Morris, a costume maker. Morris was the key to cracking the case. Not only did he sell a gorilla suit to Patterson, he gave the hoaxer tips on how to make it look more real. After watching his suit on film, the costume maker noticed that Patterson had followed his suggestions:

- Brush the fur down in the back to hide the zipper.
- Bulk up the shoulders. (Bob wore football shoulder pads.)
- Cover the area around the eyes with black makeup to hide his white skin.

Even though the eye area had been blackened, there was still a flash of light from one eye in one of the frames of the film. It was Bob's right eye — a glass eye — reflecting sunlight.

Oh, and that twisting torso glance? Morris said the gorilla head only allows the wearer to make a quarter turn. Goodbye, Bigfoot. Hello, Bobfoot.

How Not to Be Hoaxed

Suppose a friend tells you that scientists have invented a battery that will keep an iPod running forever. Even better, the technology can be used for cell phones or anything that needs a lot of power from a small battery. Come on, you want to believe him. Why would he make it up? He claims he heard it from his cousin who has a friend who worked on the battery.

Consider the hallmarks of a hoax at the beginning of this book. Does the story ring any alarm bells? If so, good thinking.

Hoaxes may have been around for a long time, but so have skeptics. William of Ockham is the skeptic's patron saint. He was an important philosopher (thinker) in the 1300s.

Ockham is best known for the idea that knowledge comes from what you experience — what you see, hear, smell, feel and taste. He thought the simplest explanation for any event is usually the best one. Other philosophers added the word *razor* to Ockham's idea. It means shaving off any unnecessary assumptions attached to an explanation.

So next time you hear something that sounds too good — or too fantastic — to be true, use your skeptic's toolbox, remember Ockham's razor, and decide if it really *is* too good to be true.

Don't be hoaxed!

entia non sunt multiplicanda praeter necessitatem

William of Ockham

Glossary

anthropologists: scientists who study humans

archaeologists: scientists who study the material remains of past human life

artifacts: ancient objects made by humans

botanists: scientists who study plant life

cyclonic wind action: wind that rotates inwards, like a tornado

deuterium: an atom that is heavier than hydrogen and useful in creating energy from fusion

epidemic: a disease that sweeps through a community making many people sick

evolution: the gradual change in plants or animals, through the process of natural selection, as they adapt to changes in the environment

fossils: the petrified remains of ancient plants or animals

missing link: in anthropology, the animal that will link humans and apes on the primate family tree

ornithologists: scientists who study birds

paleontologists: scientists who study ancient life

short-range radar: pulses of high-frequency electromagnetic waves used for finding objects

Stone Age: a prehistoric time period when people used stone tools

study skins: birds collected as scientific specimens with their insides removed

Index

Photo Credits

Pages 6 & 7 John Reader/Science Photo Library.
Page 8 top © TOPFOTO / PONOPRESSE; bottom Shutterstock.
Page 11 top © Natural History Museum, London; middle Shutterstock.
Page 12 Valerie Wyatt.
Page 13 Natasha Pitre.
Page 14 © Natural History Museum, London.
Page 15 top Hemera Technologies Inc.; bottom P. Morris/Linnean Society.
Page 17 George Shaw/Public Domain.
Page 18 courtesy T. Rowe, University of Texas at Austin.
Page 20 Shutterstock.
Pages 21, 23 & 24 John Nance.
Page 26 Robert Irving/Fortean Picture Library.
Page 27 courtesy Michael Desjardins/Greenpeace.
Page 28 left Onno Pater (Netherlands); right Fortean Picture Library.
Page 30 Gretel van Rooyen.
Page 32 Shutterstock.
Page 33 SOHO (ESA & NASA).
Page 34 Philippe Plailly/Eurelios/Science Photo Library.
Page 35 Jerry Mason/Science Photo Library.
Page 36 courtesy Brian Naranjo.
Pages 39, 40, 41 & 42 Fortean Picture Library.
Page 43 top Mark Dougan; middle Thomas Denesha;
      bottom Kathryn Hagan.
Page 44 Erik Dahinden/Fortean Picture Library.